Reincarnation - The Four Factors
4 New Ways of Looking at Reincarnation

Soul Freedom Series Vol 1

By Rise' Harrington

By Bryan Jameison, Regression Therapist 1933 - 2002

(Aka Dorgeck, Ascended Master)

Overseeing Authority – Idahohl-Adameus
(Aka St. Germain)

Rev 2.7 05/03/2018

The purpose of this book is to offer the public a new understanding of the subject of reincarnation based on the authors' personal experience and the new teachings of the Ascended Masters. We consider Reincarnation theories; entity birth and trauma Attachments, astral travel through the akashic records at pivotal historical times on earth and the occurrence of 'Walk In' lifetimes.

The Soul Freedom series of books explain how the dark forces perpetuate misinformation to control and manipulate humanity. The series is intended to offer the public easy access to an education on the specific subject that interests or troubles them with proposed solutions and understandings.

Table of Contents:

Important Note: In order to grasp the concepts discussed
here book readers will benefit by having a good
understanding of the title subject or be a somewhat
knowledgeable student of metaphysics. A glossary is
included towards the end of the book to assist novices.

Acknowledgments

I express gratitude for all of the spirit entities that attached to me throughout my life. They have provided a fuller education for the betterment of human understanding and healing. Thanks to (birth attachment) Malchor, Palestinian warrior that confused my sexual identity, while gratefully, providing me with heightened feelings of testosterone when I was threatened by male abusiveness. Thank you to my great maternal grandmother with her five attachments that forced me to find forgiveness for my own childhood molestation. I also extend acknowledgment to the (demonic) alien attachment that attempted to oppress my light for many decades. You provided me with a new perspective on the world of darkness the day I discovered and removed your presence.

My eternal gratitude to the Harrington family for a lifetime of loving support and to the Angels, Spirit Guides and Ascended Masters for exposing and fine tuning my education in the area of dark force manipulation. I feel the greatest appreciation for all of these Divine lighted ones (including humans) for backing me up and pressing me forward in order that I might prevail in bringing this darkness to light. And especially my soul mate, Dorgeck, who coaches me on these subjects and co-authors each book with loving generosity and wisdom. Now, we can make greater strides in healing our world one soul at a time.

*~ We dedicate this book to beloved
Idahohl-Adameus (St Germain) ~*

Chapter One

Reincarnation – My Theories of the Past

In 2011 I published my first book titled *Spiritual Self Mastery - Lessons on the Road to Ascension.* In this book I included a chapter on the subject of transmigration or rebirth. Several years later I removed it from the book pending development of new understandings on the philosophy of rebirth.

The following is an excerpt adapted from chapter 10 titled: *Reincarnation and Karma.*

"When I first heard of the concept of multiple lifetimes for each individual it made so much sense to me. It explained why we all come into this world with different strengths and weaknesses, varying levels of intelligence and physical qualities that can't be explained by genetics. It also makes sense of why someone is born with a fear of heights and someone else is claustrophobic. Some of us have diseases, deformities, and mental illnesses at birth and some people are artistic and intellectual geniuses. Most of us fall somewhere in between the two extremes.

In the grand scheme of creation there must be some kind of self-created karma (good and bad) in which we learn through the consequences of our choices and actions from lifetime to lifetime. If not, God would seem to be an arbitrary and uncaring creator to bless or curse each one of us randomly at birth. In actuality, God is a very kind and loving creator that gives us complete free will to choose for ourselves the lives we create. All of the less than perfect conditions in our lives are the result of our own beliefs, thoughts, choices and actions.

As we reincarnate our souls carry many unresolved problems as well as gifts & attributes from previous lifetimes into our current incarnations. Many experts in the field of reincarnation tell us that we sign up for our physical, emotional and mental challenges for the purpose of soul growth prior to birth in each lifetime. When we are in Spirit between lives we understand that the object of rebirth is to grow spiritually by balancing out the karma we incurred in past lives and to work towards fulfilling our souls purpose. It is always our choice to return to earth to atone for our actions and to choose a higher level of self-expression in the present life.

Problems we carry forward with us at birth can include unresolved emotional traumas or serious physical diseases. These unresolved issues are carried in our soul archives to be resolved in our present or future lifetime. An example of past life residue from emotional trauma brought forward to the present life might be a tragic car accident that brought sudden death to an individual. When death is sudden we don't have the necessary time to digest & process emotionally what has occurred. The result of an abrupt death may cause an individual in his/her next incarnation to be deathly afraid of driving a car. He/she may live out an entire life considering the car phobia an unreasonable fear that they'll never understand. A person afraid of heights may have jumped off a cliff to save him/her self from capture and torture in another lifetime. Suicide enacted to avoid living with a painful disease might cause a person to enter a new life with a similar disease. This would allow him/her the opportunity to face the lessons of growth the disease has to offer.

Theoretically speaking, another person may have held a position of great power over others and been dethroned or murdered. This might cause them to shy away from roles of power & leadership in a future life. It could even cause them to stifle their full expression of self and live a mediocre existence in near solitude.

Such was the case with me. In my present incarnation I have had an internal struggle going on ever since I can remember. As I grew up I felt great potential, aspirations and longings within me to create hugely for myself but I was always very shy and withholding.

I avoided attracting <u>any</u> special attention. In high school I loved to sing, dance & act in plays but always stayed within the safety of group performances. Once out of school, I dove into a career I never loved and that stifled most of my creative expression for more than 20 years. If I was singled out to give a business presentation – uncontrollable anxiety attacks prevented me from speaking. I was literally consumed by terror. As much as I longed to express the wealth of creativity and power I felt inside of me I was never able to perform singularly on any level professionally or creatively.

It wasn't until I was in my mid forty's that I decided to take action and to make some big changes in my life. I was running out of time. Hiding in the shadows was causing my life to be small, miserable and unfulfilling. My soul was suffocating - I couldn't stand to take a back seat anymore and let life move on without me.

My long-term interest and preoccupation was the study of metaphysics and spirituality. I began intensifying my metaphysical studies. I attended lectures by myself to help work through my shyness and forced myself to participate in discussions. Every morning I listened to spiritual self-help tapes to keep myself motivated and on track. I was determined to break out of the 'box' I had built and reinforced over decades.

All these things helped but I really needed something cataclysmic to break through my internal blocks. I had learned that psychological (mental & emotional) barriers were representations of fear-based beliefs.

My biggest fear was of public speaking that seemed disproportionate to the normal dread the average person feels. I had no idea why I was so terrified. I wasn't finding the answers in all the self-help books I read or tapes and lectures I listened to. I was stumped.

In the fall of 1996 I saw an advertisement in a local metaphysical magazine for a free lecture on the topic of Reincarnation. I had a gut knowing that I needed to attend. That Saturday as I drove to the lecture I was completely high wired. There was an undercurrent running through my body that was like an intuitive alarm bell sounding off. I hadn't a clue what I was getting into but I knew it was BIG.

As I sat in the audience waiting for the lecture to start I heard soft, lilting, ethereal music playing from somewhere in the background. The sounds were very faint and it seemed that the music was inside my head, audible only to me. I wondered throughout the next hour if it was my imagination or a sign from the angelic realms?

The regression therapist, Bryan Jameison, entered and began speaking informally, very casually telling us about his life and adventures while practicing Past Life Therapy for himself and others. He was very charming and humorous while relaying an important soul-healing concept. Through discovering & gaining understanding of major past life events we could find the causes of our present life imbalances. We would then be able to release the inexplicable patterns and phobias that were causing us grief in some area of our lives. I was completely sold by his message. The next day I phoned him and made an appointment for a regression therapy session.

One week later I was in session with Bryan. He used a non-hypnotic method to relax his clients. This technique brought a light trance state that opened the connection to my higher self and soul records while remaining fully alert and aware at all times.

After an hour in session we had made very little progress. I became discouraged but Bryan was determined. "Ask your higher self what lifetime is having the biggest impact on you in your present life?"

I asked the question and waited for an answer. A scene opened before me and I found myself witnessing a huge battle, frantic clashing of bodies & swords. The frenzied energy and enormity of the battle overwhelmed me. "I can't do this – no way!" I shut the scene down.

Bryan reminded me that I was revisiting a past life episode and I was in no danger now. I was fully in charge at all times. He then guided me to confirm with my higher self that I had survived that day and asked me to fast forward to the end of the battle. I found myself back on the scene sitting by myself, my back to the men of my tribe as they led prisoners away. Bryan asked a great deal of questions and we uncovered a lot about the warrior I was in that life.

We were in Palestine in the territory my tribe had inhabited and had fought many battles to keep possession of. I was the chief commander of the tribe and didn't particularly enjoy my role. I was an extremely powerful man and had little tolerance of weakness in others although I treated all members of the tribe fairly.

Bryan asked me what it was I needed to learn now from my life as the commanding warrior. The answer came quickly.

R - "There's a power struggle. I've denied myself this power because it's so big it scares the hell out of me."

B - "Why does it frighten you?"

R – I stretched my psychic antenna waiting for the answer. The answer was slow in coming. "I'm afraid to accept responsibility for being a very powerful person."

B - "Okay- now, there's a reason for that.

R – (Long pause) "The answer is… because I'll have to tend the masses again."

B – "So, if you really come into your own power – if you accept what you're capable of then, inherent with the acceptance of the power is the belief that you have to 'tend the masses again'?"

R – (Laughter)

B – "We don't' have an ego problem here…"

R – "But that's what was happening there! He had an army that followed him and the women and children to tend. It was a huge responsibility."

B – "And you don't want that this time, huh?"

R - "Right"

B – "Now where is it written that just because you've accepted your own personal power that you have to take in widows and orphans and the rest of it?"

R – (Laughter) "Oh shxx… Thank you, Bryan." I could see how ludicrous this underlying fear was and would spend a lot of time digesting what I'd learned that day. It was a lovely note to end on and I suggested we wind up our session. Bryan wasn't ready to let go yet. Even though we had uncovered an important factor in this previous life, he sensed there was more.

B – "Ok, but first ask your higher self how you met your death in that lifetime."

I was getting weary, but agreed. I returned to that soft place in the clouds and asked my higher self the final question. I didn't have to wait for an answer.

R - "I was resting under a tree. A member of my tribe snuck up on me and stuck a sword in my stomach. I was murdered."

B - "For what reason were you murdered?

R – "Jealousy."

B – "Was that over power?"

R – "Yes"

B – "So, in that lifetime you acted responsibly and you did what you had to do. You were honorable in battle, and in the end you were murdered. Ask your higher self if this has anything to do with why you have such resistance to claiming your own power. For fear, if you do, somebody will get jealous and do you in again?"

R – "Holy shxx…. What a concept, Bryan."

Of course, this was the answer I was looking for. The life of the murdered warrior was the mysterious cause of my fear of expressing myself fully. Incredibly, it's as simple as that. The answer I'd been searching for all of my adult life. This was an amazing revelation for me – that our present day psyches can be so strongly affected by past life events. The fact that these types of mystery feelings or phobias don't make sense in our present lives causes a lot of confusion for so many of us. They can so easily make us feel inadequate and powerless if left untreated.

Now that I know the cause of my unreasonable fear there is no longer a need to hide. I am reasonably confident that I won't be murdered and I can begin to express my creative self without limitation. There is greater clarity and purpose within me as I move towards the fullest expression of self I can offer in this lifetime. I will be forever grateful to Bryan for guiding me to unlock the revealing truth within me."
End of excerpt.

Was there more truth to this past lifetime as a warrior yet to be discovered? Following my session with Bryan I thought I had all of the answers that I needed.

In 2014 Chapter 10 *Reincarnation + Karma* was removed from my first book *Spiritual Self-Mastery* in its third edition. I promised that new findings coming to light were to be revealed in a future publication. See Part Two.

Chapter Two

Birth and Trauma Attachments

My Past Life Therapist, Bryan Jameison died in the year 2002 after having written four books on the subject of Reincarnation.

In the spring of 2013 I was reading *Spiritual Self Mastery* to re-familiarize myself with it. As I reached the chapter on Reincarnation I felt a strong presence accompanied by a flash of light to indicate a Spirit visitor was with me. Bryan announced his presence and expressed his pleasure at being included in the book. In this first visit it was established that he was to be my new guide on the subject of Earthbound Spirit (lost soul entity) Attachments and their troubled involvement with living humans. This training would develop over the next several years and I was very honored and pleased to have his presence guiding me.

Bryan's Spirit name is Dorgeck, meaning 'Thunderstorm of Healing'. Before he passed from earth he accomplished Ascension and is now an Ascended Master; a wise, humorous and charismatic teacher. He had learned much in the Universities of the Spirit realms since his death. His specialty of study in relation to the concept of reincarnation is lost soul entity attachments. He had developed further expertise in these areas and had some jolting revelations that would unfold over the next two years as I became ready to learn deeper truths. It was during this period that I began working on development of my second book that Dorgeck co-authored titled: *Entity Attachment Removal - Self-Help Procedure - The ABC of Releasing Spirit Attachments for Do It Yourselfers.*

During this period I was introduced to the practice of Spirit Releasement Therapy (SRT) by a Facebook association. This led me to Edith Fiore's book titled *The Unquiet Dead* in which she shares her experience with clients and what she discovered during her spirit releasement therapy sessions. I believe my jaw dropped and stayed opened through the entire reading of this book. I saw my circumstance so very clearly that I was sure it described my own condition. It was a major *light bulb* moment. My warrior memories were not a past life but actually a Spirit entity attachment that had been with me since my birth?!

Much to my surprise, Dorgeck confirmed this. He had learned the truth of the work that he had done on earth. It was not Regression Therapy to identify past lives as he had thought but that of identifying womb/birth entity attachments. Not only was this a bizarre discovery, it was even more incredible to be made aware of this by the deceased regressionist who had led me (unwittingly) to believe it was a past life. Oh my God, I thought, how much of humanity is being deceived by this kind of condition?

I did not take this discovery lightly. I just couldn't fathom how such an atrocity could occur and was upset about it for months. This man (warrior) had been inside of my mind and body causing me to feel his emotions all of my life! No wonder I have had male/female identity and emotional confusion since I was a child.

I learned that Malchor, the warriors' name, was a Spirit attachment that joined me in the womb prior to my birth. He was misguided by a group of lower sphere Spirits that were in the practice of guiding deceased human souls to over cloak (attach to) newly incepted soul births. Malchor was one of the many billions of souls that have been misdirected by this ill-informed "Reincarnation Group".

The rebirth group provides access to the Akashic records for rebirthing souls to review. As in the next chapter, we will introduce Akashic here as the record of all souls past, present and future lives and all of the potentialities within. These records are accessed for review by the rebirthing souls as living film reels reflecting life options. In Malchor's case, he would have been presented with many options of lives with the similar unhealed emotion as he carried with options that would interest him. The option that drew us together was my visit to Egypt in my mid 40s where I drew upon inspiration for the eventual creation of a Sphinx sculpture and eventual ascension Mandala painting.

Evidently, the consciousness of the Spirit group that directs the Reincarnation activities are of a low consciousness and they cannot see that there is already a new soul within the womb. The newly incepted souls' light is so pure that it can't be seen by the invading soul or the Rebirthing Group. These rebirth spirit groups are unaware of the error that they are making. See Divine Truth Video. Ref: Divine Truth - 'Spirits Who Believe in Reincarnation'. https://youtu.be/EAGbmtK696o?list=PLPBIcNBZwSjiS 2bBfonPPdOB6jla9W9ui

The Ascended Masters inform me that approximately one third of the population in the Spirit realms are misguided souls that believe in Reincarnation. The belief in rebirth was founded in the Buddhist/Hindu tradition and has grown very popular in modern times in the Western new age groups and around the world. I used to believe this was an 'enlightened' belief.

Approximately one third of the humans that die at any given time, based on their belief in the teachings of Reincarnation, may be misled to reenter an earthly body in the womb of newly incepted souls. This means that approximately 1 in 3 of every baby born to the earth has a new soul created by God's natural laws and may also have a spirit entity attachment that has over cloaked the new child in the womb. We say *may* because not all of us will desire to return to the earth regardless of our belief in Reincarnation. Free will choice is the determining factor.

----- ~0~-----

In presentation of this process we will define Birth Attachments as deceased human souls going through a *false* Reincarnation process. Our demonstration begins with a soul that has died on the earth. This soul is example number **A** we'll call Alice who died from a sudden car accident. As a result of the sudden accident she has an unhealed emotion of the fear of driving. Alice also believes in Reincarnation.

Because of Alice's belief in Reincarnation the Law Of Attraction (LOA) draws her to a group of people in the spirit realms who serve an organization with the shared belief in Reincarnation.

The people who serve in this group are ignorant souls who believe themselves to be enlightened.

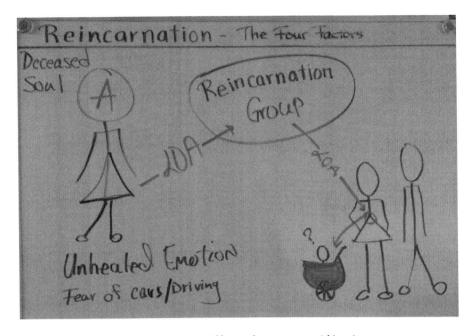

The Reincarnation group will orchestrate Alice's reentry to earth by guiding her through the LOA to the child of a parent for a myriad of reasons including similar unhealed emotion, common genetics, soul purpose etc. The soul of Alice is guided in error to over cloak the newly incepted soul within the mother.

This creates a newborn child that has an unhealed emotion inherited from Alice which will cause the child to have an unreasonable fear of cars and driving. If the child is a male he will probably also be afflicted with sexual identity confusion. This child will be likely to seek out psychological counseling and/or past life regression therapy to help understand where this fear and confusion comes from. This is when the life of Alice will be discovered and will be believed to be proof of the child's past lifetime. Indeed, this has caused lifetimes of confusion for the human race throughout history.

The other more serious consequence of Birth Attachments is disease. If Alice had died carrying a disease it would be inherited by the child within the womb and the child is born with that disease. Birth attachments account for almost all of the birth defects and diseases in newborn babies. The only exception to this is the health habits of the mother. It is for this reason that I, myself, chose to forego motherhood. In my childbearing age I was most heavily afflicted with spirit entity attachments and relied on cigarettes and alcohol abusively to cope with emotional and identity confusion that lasted for several decades.

It can be presumed that any child born with a disease or physical disfigurement has an intruding birth attachment. This is a devastating circumstance for newly born children, their parents and families.

Unless this intruding spirit entity is removed by a spiritual healer at some point in this child's young or adult life, these two personalities will share one body from birth to death for the short or long lifetime of the individual. It is my hope that enough Shamans and other spiritual healers learn about this condition that we may begin to offer healing for these newborns and their families.

Through the ongoing belief in reincarnation we are unwittingly perpetuating the spreading of disease to our newborn children over the generations caused by this false teaching.

Idahohl-Adameus (St. Germain) explains that the theory of Reincarnation was developed by the Dark Forces as a method to cheapen life and to further control and manipulate humanity. *If we believe* we have many, many lifetimes to correct past misdeeds then perhaps we can be forgiven in a later lifetime for raping and killing our brothers and sisters in the present life with little or no justification.

Note: We are <u>not</u> suggesting that the Buddhist/Hinduism traditions were created by the Dark Forces or that they are greatly influenced by them. It is only the one belief system (Reincarnation) that is the concern.

I was able to remove and cross over my spirit intruder, Malchor, with the guidance of my Spirit Team. It wasn't easy to convince him to leave because when a soul has been in a body for many decades he/she is comfortable. He did not want to be uprooted. But it was necessary for him in order for his own soul to continue to grow spiritually and to enable me to progress spiritually with soul autonomy.

Months after crossing him over to the Spirit realms Dorgeck brought Malchor to my attention. I was advised that he was hiding in the darkest regions of the Spirit realm because he couldn't forgive himself for what he had done to me. Malchor carried this guilt even though he had been falsely instructed to enter into my birthing chamber by then there spirits of false authority. Of course, I instantly forgave him and assured him of this. He was greatly relieved and immediately brightened, offering to help guide me in the future development of the Sphinx project should I choose to move ahead with it.

What a treat that was, to make an alliance and supportive friend with one who was once a very unwelcome Spirit intruder!

--------------------------- ~ 0 ~ ----------------------

Trauma Attachments

There is another factor considering attachments that we need to address. This is the circumstance of **Trauma Attachments.** It is a subject we cover in some detail in *Entity Removal - Self-Help* Procedure - The ABC of Releasing Spirit Attachments **for *Do It Yourselfers** -Soul Freedom Series Vol 3*. People with unhealed emotional trauma attract entity attachments with similar unhealed emotions based on the universal Law of Attraction (LOA).

I will use myself as an example. I carried an unhealed emotional trauma caused by a molestation experience at the age of four. Through the LOA I experienced an attachment at age 5 by a woman entity with the same unhealed emotion. Consequently from the age of five onward I had dreams and vague memories of other souls that included my birth attachment (Malchor) and the other female soul attached through my unhealed emotional trauma. Lost souls that attach to us throughout our lives due to serious emotional traumas are also a factor that may lead us to search for present day psychological influences or mislead us to search for past life identities.

Chapter Three

Historical Lifetimes - Astral Travel through the Akashic Records

Akashic Records are the thoughts, emotions and wisdom of all souls including their past, present, and probable future. The Library of the Akashic is where all souls' Records are stored in the higher frequency realms of consciousness. These records are seen by some as endless golden corridors of books and others as living film reels reflecting life options.

There is another category in human experience that might masquerade as a past life. We can describe this as a *sleeping* Astral Hitchhiker. These are dreams of historical life memories in which our Guidance teams lead us into the past through the Akashic records during important times in history. Through this sleeping astral travel we may gain experience from pivotal times in the past of historical figures. I personally have hitchhiked or temporarily walked in the shoes of Joan of Arc and Guinevere of Camelot. How many of my earthborn sister's, throughout time, have also had memories of these historical personalities' lives? And how many have astral hitchhiked to share in the life of Jesus, Cleopatra or Mother Mary? The list of possibilities is endless.

Dorgeck speaks to this issue from his position in the realms of spirit.

"I have been trained in other aspects of reincarnation and it is multifaceted in its seeming reality. There are many hidden realms of information over the centuries and millennia that have been drawn from the Akashic records to fulfill the desire to have lived in different times. This is because it's been implanted in our souls at inception that we may become aware of evolutionary processes that were accomplished over time, you see."

"This ties in the history as you have been aware of yourself in our Camelot connection, beloved, although we have not been specifically incarnated into those positions."

So if we take this somewhat enigmatic explanation we may interpret it to mean: As part of our souls purpose, at inception, the Divine Hierarchy implants a seed within us that will flower at some time in our life. This seed initiates divinely guided exposure to astral travel through the Akashic records. This enables us to experience a time in the past through a key player. This important figure is relevant to what we need to learn to enhance our soul assets and to eventually fulfill the specific purpose in our lifetime. It is like a training ground for the soul to prepare for our own life purpose that may include similar dynamics. I astral traveled, escorted by my

Spirit Guidance, to the time of Camelot as Guinevere and joined with Dorgeck who was hitchhiking as the personality of King Arthur.

Hundreds of years later, in 1996, when I met Dorgeck as my past life regressionist, Bryan Jameison, my soul memory recognized him as someone that was a major player in my life. I intuitively recognized him although I was not then aware of the historical Camelot connection. The soul recognition and attraction was immediate and incredibly strong. 10 years following Bryan Jameison's death in present time it was this soul bond that enabled my spiritual reconnection to Dorgeck to feel meaningful and synchronistically purposeful.

Dorgeck suggests that we should each work with our guidance to reveal the historical astral journeys we may have taken through the Akashic records. We need to remember and release the memories of these historical lifetimes so that we may be clear within our own soul records who it is we truly are. The old memories may be released in meditations (with guidance assisting) so that you can **retain** only the lessons learned from the historical life and own the soul assets that were gained to enhance your life's path.

We should also ask our guidance team if there is any unresolved emotional healing within our souls from the Akashic record experience. This will need to be addressed and healed in meditation also. An example of this is that we may have relationship with someone that was simply a fellow hitchhiker in Akashic historical relationship where there may have seemed to be an unforgivable transgression between us. This means that it is possible to hold a grudge for someone in our present life relationships without understanding why. I will use my own life experience hitchhiking in Camelot as an example:

Guinevere and King Arthur's marriage was broken for a time when she rendezvoused with Sir Lancelot. It was during this time when Dorgeck and I astral traveled through the Akashic temporarily. We were not present in the time period of Akashic history when Guinevere later reconciled and reunited with King Arthur. Because he was unaware of the healing between them Dorgeck still carried the unhealed emotion within his own soul of non-forgiveness for Guinevere. This caused us both to experience unnecessary turmoil hundreds of years later. In present time Dorgeck cautions us to be nakedly honest with ourselves to determine if we may be retaining unhealed emotions. Our Spirit Guides and Angels will help us to uncover this in our meditative work when we ask for their help.

Because of the above scenario we need to ask our Angels and Spirit Guides to assist us in forgiving our own transgressions that occurred in our historical Akashic life memories. This will ensure that we do not carry the grievance forward in our soul records.

The deeds of our fellow dream travelers should not be held accountable for transgressions conducted as an astral hitchhiker, regardless of the outcome.

--------- ~ 0 ~ -------

Chapter Four

Walk In Lifetimes – Serving the Highest Good

Idahohl-Adameus (St Germain) assures me that beings of the Spiritual Hierarchy orchestrate newly incepted soul births under the laws of the Higher Orders and that the new souls do have Divine consciousness within them. This Divine intelligence is aware of itself and is in agreement with its' purpose in pre-soul inception. Then it is true that we do agree with our souls' purpose prior to our birth and all is in Divine Order.

This last example of quasi past lifetime experiences is termed 'Walk-In'. Walk-Ins are always orchestrated by the Spiritual Hierarchy before a new souls' inception. Prior to birth, the soul that is being born agreed to a soul swap out with a spiritually enlightened being at an agreed upon point in their life. The two souls swap out during a time of unconsciousness by the original incarnate soul. The loss of consciousness may happen during an a peaceful sleep exchange, an illness or an accident.

The spiritually enlightened soul merges into the brain and body of the original host soul through the bottom of the skull (medulla oblongata) during the soul swap process. The original soul exits simultaneously through the same place at the back of the head and base of the skull. As a result of this trade the now enlightened soul gains all of the original souls educational training and memories. Suffice it to say that the end result is new skill sets, inherent wisdom and power displayed in the human personality. This will enable the person in this position to fulfill the purpose of critically important assignments on earth for the Highest Good of all.

I can speak personally to this as I experienced being a Walk-In at a pivotal point in earth's history. I swapped out with a young man who had the significant position of Jesus' cousin, John the Baptist. The young man who was John was not strong enough to adequately herald the Master Jesus.

As a Walk-In I merged with the brain of the young adult John. This must have been quite an adjustment to Walk-In at this time in history but I have little memory of it. I have been given only key memory points and visions. The clearest memory is of being strangled to death by King Herod prior to being beheaded.

I use myself as an example here only because I am instructed to do so by guidance and I trust that it is for the highest good in a way I cannot now see.

----- ~0~ -----

John the Baptist – Soul Fragmentation – My Story –

The physical sign of this unhealed emotion started as a small blemish at my right temple. I follow Louise Hayes *Heal Your Body* philosophy: *The Mental Causes for Physical Illness and the Metaphysical Way to Overcome Them*. As soon as the small blemish became an obvious sign of imbalance within me I began a healing journey that lasted over 2 years. I healed everything in my physical, mental and spiritual past and after a year and a half it was still growing. After having confirmed with my Angels that my soul was free of any damage from my current life, it was time for a final desperate meditation.

I had learned about soul fragmentation and retrieval many years ago. (We cover this subject in more detail in Soul Freedom Vol-3). My prior inquiries about soul fragments were not revealed to me when I asked previously because I was not ready to face the reality and enormity of the fragmentation to be healed.

As John the Baptist I was locked in a dungeon and repeatedly sodomized by the Roman guards as ordered by King Herod. The magnitude of soul wretchedness I endured repeatedly caused multiple soul fragmentations. I was shackled at the neck and wrists which disabled my ability to commit suicide.

2000 years later, it was now necessary to undergo the process of forgiveness for the ones that committed repeated humiliation and torment to a defenseless human being. I imagined the blackest soul desolation, self-loathing and disregard for life that was the reality for these ones. This realization caused compassion to flow out from me. Forgiveness came very naturally and easily as I felt the compassionate truth of their individual soul deprivation.

Once forgiveness was completed I had an amazing revelation. The part of my soul that was John was still in the dungeon from 2000 years ago!

I called for Christ Light healing and release from the dungeon. There was a huge, experiential, golden burst of starlight that illuminated my inner vision with John flying out of the dungeon, soaring upward to reunite with me! And I was returned to wholeness.

And today, the temple tumor, after 2 years has mushroomed out to 1 inch round, turned bright red and become shaped like a heart. I am reminded that it is all about love and that love heals all things. I now witness it becoming severed at points of the core as it begins the process of releasing itself from my face. Hallelujah!

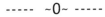

I will state the obvious. I am making an exception of myself when I say there is no reincarnation. AJ Miller (Aka Jesus) presents the claim that only 14 individuals have ever reincarnated on earth due to Divine Intelligence or Spiritual Hierarchy exception. I am not sure about that claim as I believe there may be more than this, myself being one of them. If I had not incarnated prior to my current lifetime I would not have existed in the Spirit Realms in order to Walk-In to John the Baptist.

On a personal note, I have a mixed opinion of the character John the Baptist. John brought on his own imprisonment and execution by publicly and repeatedly denouncing King Herod's infidelity. It seems to me that he was a judgmental and religious fanatic that did adequately fulfill the purpose of heralding master Jesus.

----- ~O~ -----

I asked Dorgeck how many Walk-Ins currently exist on earth as I suspected it to be enormous. I have been amazed for many years at how many spiritual teachers, speakers and enlightened ones are appearing around the globe. We will close the subject of Walk-Ins with Dorgeck's words:

"We would suggest that there are so many Walk-Ins upon the earth that it would not be conceivable to count them all. These are pivotal times upon the earth, as you know. As we ride the wave to the Aquarian age there will be even more Walk-Ins to expand the light frequencies upon the earth so that we can finally, finally assist our mother Earth in Ascension, indeed."

Chapter Five

The Enlightening Truth of AJ Miller (A.K.A. Jesus)

I spent a full year in a self-imposed internship as a medium performing Angel readings and Spirit attachment removals. I did not charge for these services but gained a lot of very valuable experience. While working with clients I found most entity attachments were caused by unhealed emotions from childhood traumas. These unhealed emotional traumas created holes in the aura and soul fragment loss. The Law of Attraction drew lost soul entities with similar unhealed emotions to attach to the human, exacerbating the problem and causing havoc in the humans life. It was during this period that I began writing my second book *Entity Removal - Self-Help Procedure - The ABC of Releasing Spirit Attachments for Do It Yourselfers - Soul Freedom Series Vol 3*
Book Link: http://www.amazon.com/Soul-Freedom-Earthbound-Attachment-ebook/dp/B00EESYNIY/ This book can be referenced for further understanding on the subject of entity attachments and hauntings.

Note: The principle of attachment based on the Law of Attraction is different when applied to a newly incepted baby soul. A newly incepted soul does not have an unhealed emotion but the parent does. In this case, the Law of Attraction draws the Spirit entity to the baby of the _parent_ with a similar unhealed emotion. *See the clarification on this in the concluding section of this chapter.

In my case, the warrior Malchor was drawn to the unhealed emotion of my father. That emotion was a terror of being murdered which I do not remember ever seeing any evidence of during my father's life time except for the heavy alcohol addiction that I also became susceptible to.

I began studying the teachings of AJ Miller (a.k.a. Jesus) in 2013 because I resonated to the truths that he spoke about spiritual laws. It wasn't until I listened to his December 2015 videotaped sessions that I had the corroboration needed for my own discovery and suspicion about Reincarnation. AJ's statements of truth along with his videotaped discussions with Spirit entities promoting rebirth have firmly grounded me in the debunking of Reincarnation teachings. And of course, the Ascended Masters concur with AJ's teachings on this subject.

Ref video Divine Truth 20151222 – 1230 New Age Philosophies - At 52 minutes starts a discussion on 'Human Belief in Reincarnation'. There are two main reasons presented in this video that substantiates belief in Reincarnation for many people: 1. People are generally afraid to die. It is a relief to know/believe that we get another opportunity to live again and potentially correct the mistakes we made in the most recent life. 2. People witness newborn babies in the same family with similar personality traits of someone who previously died. It is often believed this is a reincarnation of the previously deceased family member. In essence this is potentially true as grandpa may be wrongly instructed to over cloak (attach to) his own newborn grandchild. Note: According to Ascended Master guidance the naturally intended 'host' soul of the physical body will always be the primary soul and dominating personality over the intruding soul entity attachment. In this example the child will have grandpa's influence and some characteristics but grandpa will not be the dominating personality.

I strongly encourage readers to expand your understandings and awareness based on the evidence in this presentation and the videos below. Perhaps you will be able to experience new realizations of truth on the subject of Reincarnation as I did.

'Spirits Who Believe in Reincarnation'. This features a group of misinformed Spirits and their dismay at being proven to be in error about their practices of guiding humans into the false practice of Reincarnation.
Ref video: Divine Truth 20151223 - 1230 (Spirits in First Sphere)
Link: https://youtu.be/EAGbmtK696o

'Spirits Who Exploit People on Earth.' This video tape describes many ways in which malevolent Spirits manipulate humans and includes the concept of reincarnation exploitation.
Ref video: Divine Truth 20151223 – 1500 (Spirits in First Sphere)
Link: https://youtu.be/uwGi4KT1khs

What is Spirit influence, attachment, over-cloaking & possession? AJ discusses the Spirit attachment process by the intruding reincarnation entity within the first 5 minutes of this video. He covers attachments in other circumstances throughout the video. Ref video: Divine Truth 20130819 - FAQ Series
Link:
https://youtu.be/Y4e8BlvpUIo?list=PLPBIcNBZwSjiS2 bBfonPPdOB6jla9W9ui

-------- Concluding Argument -------

How much of the world's suffering is related to Spirit influence?
Ref video: Divine Truth 20130819 FAQ Series
https://www.youtube.com/watch?v=macpVWYww0

Statement - AJ says in this video that all of our suffering is caused by our own choices to act out of harmony with love. Our choices attract Spirit influence for the negative or positive.

Author's Question - New born babies: If we are newly incepted souls attached to at birth by a Spirit who is drawn to our parental condition with a similar unhealed emotion, this is not the choice of the child. The new child grows up under the influence of an unwell Spirit attachment. This seems to be an unfair start with an unclean slate for the newborn child. It is not the choice of the child to act out of harmony with love. Why does a child have to suffer from the unhealed emotion of the parent? If karma and reincarnation are not the justifying force - what is?

Answer - Following meditation on this subject, these are my realizations. Jesus has always said that we should learn from the child, be as the child. The light of the newborn is pure even with an attachment. It is the newborn that shines unscarred, Christ consciousness unaffected. Each parent has the opportunity to experience a rebirth in relation to this child and the childrearing. Each of us has the opportunity to evolve in this circumstance. I saw/felt a unity of collective consciousness acting out spiritual evolvement through the generations, synchronistically balancing, harmonizing and spiraling into the oneness of our Creator.

Author's note: I have not yet found peace with this circumstance but I do have faith that it will *eventually* be resolved with the education and evolvement of human consciousness. I also have extraordinary faith in the ultimate Divine Order of our Creators' universe.

----- ❧ *End* ❧ -----

Glossary

Akashic: The Akashic Records are the thoughts, emotions and wisdom of all souls including their past, present, and probable future. The Library of the Akashic is where all souls' records are stored in higher frequency realms of consciousness. These records are seen by some as endless golden corridors of books and others as living film reels reflecting life options.

Anorexia: An emotional disorder characterized by an obsessive desire to lose weight by refusing to eat. If a man person is afflicted by dark entity or Demon attachment there may be an inability to eat as normal.

Ascended Masters: When a soul's purpose is to achieve Ascended Mastery he/she is guided through much strife and determination to achieve Self Mastery in one lifetime on earth. The purpose of this is to enlighten the world and be a blessing to the earth for the highest good of all.

Astral: 1) *Common:* Of or relating to a supposed nonphysical realm of existence to which various psychic and paranormal phenomena are ascribed, and in which the physical human body is said to have an etheric counterpart. 2) *Soul Freedom:* The astral realm is as an atmospheric spirit environment surrounding the earth and all of the universe. It is a field of travel between spheres of consciousness in spirit. It is also used to temporarily house the human souls/spirits that become lost or stuck in the death transition from earth to the Spirit Realm.

Dimension: Vibration - Earth is three-dimensional, the Astral realm is fourth dimensional, the Spirit Realm is fifth dimensional. There may be many spheres of consciousness with in a dimensional realm.

Divination: The practice of seeking knowledge of the future or the unknown by supernatural means.

Elohim: God/Goddess's creator Angels.

Entity: Used in the context of this book to mean a Spirit being without a physical body of its own. A Spirit soul personality.

Esoteric: Intended for or likely to be understood by only a small number of people with a specialized knowledge or interest, or an enlightened inner circle.

Etheric body: The "human energy field" or aura, Aka Spirit body.

Illuminati: A secret society of people believed to be of very dark intent controlling the earth politically and financially in order to rule the world.

Mandala: A spiritual and ritual symbol in Hinduism and Buddhism used for meditation.

Medulla Oblongata: Indented hollow at the back of the head and base of the skull.

Possession: State of taking over complete control of a persons' mind and body.

Reincarnation: The rebirth of a soul in a new body.

Satanic: Extremely evil or wicked, diabolical and fiendish.

Shaman: A person having access to, and influence in, the world of good Spirits that are accessed with the purpose of divination and healing for the Earth and humanity.

Shape Shift: The ability to change one's self from one shape into that of an animal or another type of human being.

Soul: The spiritual or immaterial part of a human being regarded as immortal and retaining all soul records throughout the souls eternity.

Soul Retrieval: The work of a healer working in the world of Spirit to retrieve a fragment of another's soul and to reintegrate into their soul.

Sphere: Spiritual level of consciousness

Spirit Releasement Therapists: (SRT) Treatment coined by William J Baldwin PH.D. who trains medical and mental health professionals to heal clients from entity attachments and possessions by removing the invading entities.

Spirit: The author's definition: The God/Goddess life force that carries the consciousness, body and soul.

Vibration: Vibration is the emanation of consciousness (as energy) in varying degrees of light or dark. How we think, eat and behave is impressed upon the personal energy that we radiate (vibrate). If we were measured, as an average, most of us would range in vibration between varying shades of grayish colors – not light or dark, but somewhere in between.

Walk-In: Prior to birth a new soul agrees to a soul swap out with a spiritually enlightened being at an agreed upon point in their life. The purpose of this is to affect significant change at pivotal times in Earth's history for the highest good of all concerned.

Witchcraft: The practice of creating magic spells to affect a person's life or that of another for good or for evil.

Bibliography

*Note: Books on the subjects of Spirit Release Therapy and Demons are included in the bibliography as research reference material only. I do not necessarily recommend or agree with their ideas, statements or practices.

Anatomy of the Spirit – The Seven Stages of Power and Healing by Caroline Myss, PhD

Angel Therapy – Healing Messages for Every Area of Your Life by Doreen Virtue Ph.D.

Arcturian Songs of the Masters of Light by Patricia Pereira

Autobiography of a Yogi by Paramahansa Yogananda

The Book of Knowledge: The Keys of Enoch® by J.J. Hurtak 1977

The Celestine Prophecy by James Redfield

Close Encounters of the Possession Kind by William J Baldwin, PhD

The Complete Ascension Manual – How to Achieve Ascension in This Lifetime by Joshua David Stone, Ph.D

The Dream Book - Symbols for Self Understanding by Betty Bethards

Emissary of Light: A Vision of Peace by James F. Twyman

Entity Removal - Self-Help Procedure - The ABC of Releasing Spirit Attachments for Do It Yourselfers - Soul Freedom Series Vol 3 by Rise' Harrington and Bryan Jameison

Exorcism for Light Workers -The Loving Way to Exorcise Evil - Soul Freedom Vol 2 by Rise' Harrington and Bryan Jameison

Exploring Your Past Lives (1976) by Bryan Jameison

Family of Light: Pleiadian Tales and Lessons in Living by Barbara Marciniak

A Field Guide to Demons - Theories, Fallen Angels, and Other Subversive Spirits by Carol K. Mack and Dinah Mack (Interesting reading but I, Rise' Harrington, believe most of this book is based only on myths)

Heal Your Body - The Mental Causes for Physical Illness and the Metaphysical Way to Overcome Them by Louise Hay

Healing Lost Souls - Releasing Unwanted Spirits from Your Energy Body by William J Baldwin, PhD

Healing With the Angels - How the Angels Can Assist You in Every Area of Your Life by Doreen Virtue

The Highly Sensitive Person's Survival Guide: Essential Skills for Living Well in an Overstimulating World (Step-By-Step Guides) by Ted Zeff and Elaine N. Aron

Left To Tell - Discovering God Amidst the Rwandan Holocaust by Immaculee Ilibagiza

Love Without End - Jesus Speaks by Glenda Green

The Power of Now by Eckhart Tolle

The Ptaah Tapes: Transformation of the Species by *Jani King and P'Taah*

Radical Forgiveness - Making Room for the Miracle by Colin C. Tipping

Reincarnation - The Four Factors - Soul Freedom Series Vol 1 by Rise' Harrington and Bryan Jameison

The Search for Past Lives (2002) by Bryan Jameison

Shamanism for Beginners by James Endredy

Siddhartha by Hermann Hesse

Songs Of Malantor: The Arcturian Star Chronicles Volume Three by Patricia L. Pereira and Sue Mann

Soul Retrieval - Mending the Fragmented Self by Sandra Ingerman

Spiritual Self Mastery - Lessons on the Road to Ascension

by Rise' Harrington and Bryan Jameison

The Unquiet Dead – A Psychologist Treats Spirit Possession by Dr. Edith Fiore

Website: www.DivineTruth.com by AJ Miller (AJ discusses Lost Soul Entity Attachment in videos throughout his website). The term he uses for spirit attachments is "over cloaking".

You Are Psychic – The Art Of Clairvoyant Reading and Healing by Debra Lynne Katz

About the Author

Medium and Author Rise' (Resa) Harrington has developed universally shared spiritual teachings from her own life experiences. This includes the uphill climb with birth and trauma entity attachments, identity confusion, childhood sexual molestation and multiple Demonic possession attempts. Her material is expanded by the shared experiences with thousands of people in her readership and Mediumship practice.

Rise's life challenges, spiritual studies and Angel guidance have enabled her to develop her own successful healing processes that culminated in the publication of her first book *Spiritual Self Mastery - Lessons on the Road to Ascension*. This book documents the path that Rise' developed in the resolution of her entity attachments as she rose from the darkness into the light, growing vibrationally through the years beyond reach of the dark and Demonic factors. This makes her an effective mentor and healer for people at all levels to raise themselves vibrationally in the same manner and begin to evolve into their highest expressions of soul self.

Rise' received higher metaphysical instruction and guidance from her Angels, Spirit Guides and the Ascended Masters. She has since become merged with her soul group of 11 other members and is now an earth-based member of this higher dimensional soul group called Evian. Soul mate Dorgeck co-authors her books as Bryan Jameison, his original incarnation name.

Rise' has practiced mediumship focused on assisting the Lost Soul population in the Astral realms since 1999. She went public in her Mediumship Practice in 2013 offering Diagnostic Readings for Lost Soul Entity Haunting, Attachment and Demonic Possession with recommended treatments. She also offers Spiritual Mentoring from her Facebook groups *Mediums Are Empaths Empowered* and *Spiritual Self-Mastery*. Rise' provides Angel and Spirit Guide readings from her website GuideLights.org. All links listed below.

Rise's spiritual life path has been greatly influenced by her 20 years of mostly career related world travels to the Far East, Europe and Egypt. Rise' is a certified Medium and a Minister of the Universal Life Church. She has been channeling St Germain privately for more than15 years and most recently has begun publicly channeling his higher self Spirit name Idahohl-Adameus.

She was raised in Los Gatos, California and now resides in San Diego County California.

Contact: riseguidelights@gmail.com
Web: http://guidelights.org

Facebook:
http://www.facebook.com/rise.harrington

Facebook Group:
https://www.facebook.com/groups/MediumsAreEmpath/ *Mediums Are Empaths Empowered*

Facebook Group:
https://www.facebook.com/groups/Spiritual.Self.Mastery/ *Spiritual Self Mastery – Lessons on the Road to Ascension*

Facebook Page:
https://www.facebook.com/Idahohl.Adameus.STGermain
Idahohl - Adameus - Saint Germain

Facebook Page:
http://www.facebook.com/EntityRemovalTreatment

Soul Freedom -
Healing From Earthbound Spirit Attachment

78263195R00031

Made in the USA
Middletown, DE
01 July 2018